A Prophetic Diary
Companion to

The Chosen Leah

Copyright © 2025 by Leah VaDol Kirk

All rights are reserved, and no part of this publication may be reproduced, distributed, or transmitted in any manner, whether through photocopying, recording, or any other electronic or mechanical methods, without the explicit prior written permission of the publisher. This restriction applies to any form or means of reproduction or distribution.

Exceptions to this rule include brief quotations that may be incorporated into critical reviews, as well as certain other noncommercial uses that are allowed by copyright law. Any such usage must adhere to the specified conditions and permissions outlined by the copyright holder.

Book Design by HMDPublishing.com

Website: www.leahvadolkirk.com
Instagram: @the.chosen.leah
Facebook: Leah VaDol

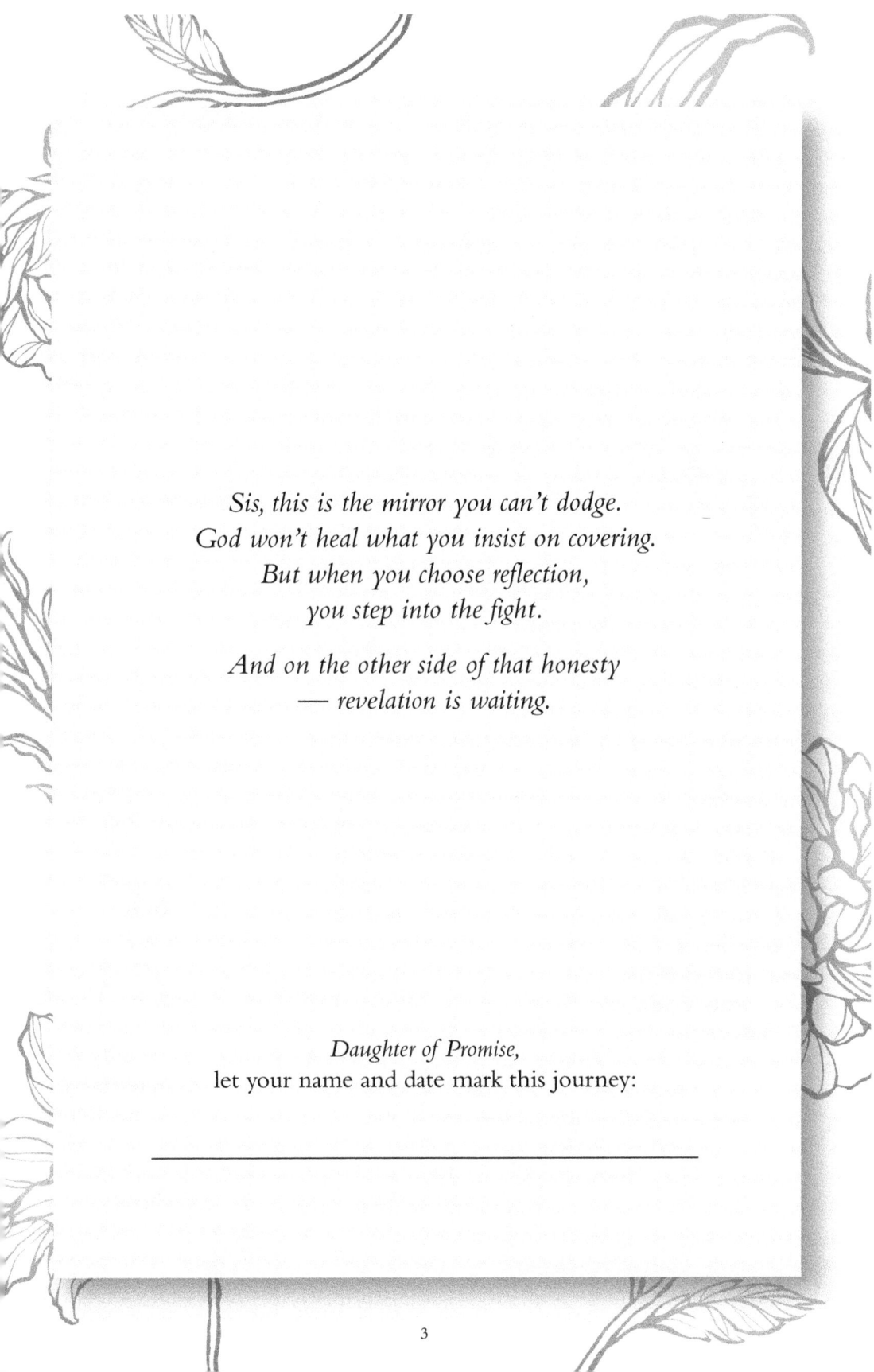

Sis, this is the mirror you can't dodge.
God won't heal what you insist on covering.
But when you choose reflection,
you step into the fight.

And on the other side of that honesty
— revelation is waiting.

Daughter of Promise,
let your name and date mark this journey:

_____

My Dear Sister,

This is not just another journal you picked up to scribble in when you feel like it. This is a prophetic companion — and I'm walking with you through these pages.

From the very first word, I need you to understand: this work is not for the faint of heart. These reflections will not let you hide. They will press on your wounds until you stop calling them healed. They will confront the places you've been covering and dare you to bring them into the light of God's presence. This diary is not a space to gloss over what hurts; it's where you'll let Him do the surgery only He can do.

But hear me — you cannot rush this. Transformation is not microwaved. If you try to fly through, you will cheat yourself out of the breakthrough. This is one day at a time. For some chapters, it might even be one week at a time. That's okay. Go at the pace your healing demands. The point is not finishing quickly — it's finishing honestly.

And honesty is the key here. Vulnerability and transparency aren't optional; they're the price of admission. If you give this halfway, you'll get halfway. If you give this everything, you'll find God waiting at the bottom of your truth with His promises intact.

I am not just the name on the spine of this book; I am your companion through every reflection. My voice will meet you here with prophetic weight and millennial sass, because I refuse to let you cover up what God is ready to uncover. I'll cheer you on and challenge you in the same breath. I'll remind you that you're chosen, even when you don't feel it. And I'll hold the mirror steady when you want to look away.

So don't skim. Don't fake it. Don't quit. Take your time. Write it raw. Let your Sacred Reflections become the revelation that carries you into victory.

With love and fire,
Leah VaDol Kirk

The Sacred Path

Each Diary Encounter corresponds to the matching chapter in The Chosen Leah

The Blueprint 6

THE OLD TESTAMENT: THE BECOMING
01. Diary Encounter: Sacred Reflection 1 10
02. Diary Encounter: Sacred Reflection 2 15
03. Diary Encounter: Sacred Reflection 3 21
04. Diary Encounter: Sacred Reflection 4 27
05. Diary Encounter: Sacred Reflection 5 33
06. Diary Encounter: Sacred Reflection 6 39

THE NEW TESTAMENT: THE FULFILLMENT
07. Diary Encounter: Sacred Reflection 7 46
08. Diary Encounter: Sacred Reflection 8 52
09. Diary Encounter: Sacred Reflection 9 58
10. Diary Encounter: Sacred Reflection 10 64
11. Diary Encounter: Sacred Reflection 11 70
12. Diary Encounter: Sacred Reflection 12 78

The Blueprint

These pages were crafted to carry more than ink — they carry encounter. This journal is not just for writing, it is for meeting. Each page invites you closer, every reflection becomes a conversation with God. Every entry carries purpose beyond the page. This diary is a prophetic companion — a map, a mirror, and a meeting place with the Almighty. Each entry you walk through is called a **Diary Encounter: Sacred Reflection**. That name is intentional.

- **Diary** — because this is intimate. Raw. Unfiltered. Your story written in your own hand.
- **Encounter** — because every reflection is not just about looking inward but meeting the living God in those places.
- **Sacred Reflection** — because this is where your honesty becomes holy, where your words turn into revelation.

Most Diary Encounters follow a seven-fold rhythm — not because numbers save you, but because the number seven carries prophetic weight. Seven speaks of completion, divine order, and God's glory made visible. This rhythm is a way to mirror His patterns as you move through your own becoming and fulfillment.

1. **Reflection Hook** — a question or challenge that shakes the mask and gets real.
2. **Season Discernment** — space to locate yourself in God's timing and your current posture.
3. **Deep Dig Prompts** — where you write what you'd rather avoid. The uncomfortable questions that heal.
4. **Prophetic Declaration Space** — because once you've named the pain, you must also prophesy the promise.
5. **Scripture Anchors** — verses that hold you steady, with guidance to activate them in your own life.

6. **Bonus Healing Exercises / Fulfillment Practices** — simple acts or reflections that help you embody the Becoming arc (healing) or the Fulfillment arc (stewardship).
7. **Prophetic Prayer for Your Becoming / Fulfillment** — my prayer over you, tailored to the season you're walking through, so you never leave a Diary Encounter without a word spoken over your spirit.

Not every Diary Encounter will look identical. Some will stretch the pattern, some will carry lighter or heavier weight depending on the chapter. But this rhythm is the backbone of the journey.

This is your blueprint. This is how you will write your way into healing, wrestle your way into identity, and declare your way into promise. Every page is designed to meet you where you are, but not leave you there.

The Old Testament: The Becoming

Sacred Reflections 1-6

This is the wilderness stretch — the sacred space where masks are stripped and wounds surface, where God teaches you who you are before He ever shows you what you'll hold. Don't rush this part. Sit with it. Breathe through it. Let Him refine you, because everything He uncovers, He intends to redeem.

Becoming is not punishment; it's preparation. It's the pruning that makes room for fruit. It's the mirror that feels too honest, yet sets you free. Here, God chisels away survival patterns so He can reveal true identity. Here, pain becomes seed, and seed becomes testimony.

And know this: your pace may look different than someone else's. Some healing happens quickly, and some unfolds slowly over years — both are holy. The goal is not speed but surrender, because God is faithful to finish what He starts in you.

This section of Sacred Reflections is about telling the truth of your sacred mess, discerning your season, and letting your story be met by His story. Write raw. Write slow. Write brave. Because every layer you surrender in becoming is the soil where your promise will take root.

— Prophetic Declaration —

"This is my season of becoming. I will not despise the wilderness or the work of healing. I choose to face what I've hidden, to name what has hurt me, and to walk in truth. I trust that every layer God reveals He will redeem. My becoming is not punishment; it is preparation, and I will come out of this season whole."

DIARY ENCOUNTER:
Sacred Reflection 1

*(Aligned with Chapter 1 of The Chosen Leah —
Finding Leah, The Season of Self & Sacred Mess)*

1. Reflection Hook

Sis, don't play with me right now. Where did you first learn to put on the mask? Who told you that you had to hold it all together when your world was falling apart? Write it down. God can't heal what you keep hiding.

....

....

....

....

2. Season Discernment

Circle the season that feels most true to you right now — and don't sugarcoat it:

- **Wilderness** — lost, searching, unraveling
- **Healing** — bandaging wounds, learning to let go
- **Becoming** — stepping into who God called you to be
- **Promise** — walking in fulfillment and covenant

Now, write why you chose this season. What evidence do you see in your life right now that points to it?

....
....
....
....
....

3. Deep Dig Prompts

This is where the surface answers won't cut it. Get uncomfortable — that's where the healing is.

- *What part of your story feels like "a sacred mess"? (That place where it's both tragic and holy.)*

....
....
....
....
....

- *Where have you been pretending you're fine, but you're actually still fractured?*

....
....
....
....
....

- *If you peeled back the layers, what would the 16-year-old you still be crying out for today?*

....
....
....
....
....

4. Prophetic Declaration Space

Now that you've been honest about the broken places, it's time to speak life into them. Begin with this declaration, then expand it in your own words:

> *"Even here, in the wilderness, God sees me. I will not be forgotten. I will not be abandoned. My sacred mess is becoming my sacred testimony."*

Add your own declarations. Name your healing, your becoming, your promise. Prophesy over yourself until your heart believes it.

....
....
....
....
....

5. Scripture Anchors

Genesis 29:31 — *"When the Lord saw that Leah was not loved, he enabled her to conceive…"*

☞ God saw Leah's rejection and moved in power anyway. He gave her the ability to birth in the very place she felt unloved.

In your life, where have you felt unseen or unwanted — and what has God been quietly producing in that hidden place?

....
....
....
....
....

Psalm 147:3 — *"He heals the brokenhearted and binds up their wounds."*

☞ This is not a poetic metaphor; it's a binding covenant promise. God doesn't just notice your pain — He commits Himself to heal it.

What wounds are you still carrying that you've never let Him bind up? Write them here and ask Him to do what only He can do.

....
....
....
....
....

BONUS HEALING EXERCISE

Laying Down the Mask

This is your chance to make the invisible visible. On the left side, write down the "masks" you've worn to survive: the roles, performances, fake smiles, or perfectionist fronts you've used to hide the pain. On the right side, write the truths God says about you — the real identity underneath the mask.

When you finish, cross out each mask with a single bold line and speak this out loud:

> *"I lay down the mask. I pick up my true identity in Christ."*

Masks I've Worn	Truth About Who I Am
....	....
....	....
....	....
....	....
....	....
....	....

Prophetic Prayer for Your Becoming

Father, I thank You for my sister who has chosen courage over comfort and vulnerability over silence. You see the sacred mess she carries — every hidden fracture, every mask she has worn just to survive. I pray she would know that You are not repelled by her brokenness, but drawn to it. Where she has felt unseen, let her feel Your gaze. Where she has felt unloved, let her know she is cherished. Where she has carried shame, let her encounter Your glory.

Turn her wilderness into a meeting place with You. Breathe life over every place that feels abandoned, and remind her that her sacred mess is becoming her sacred testimony. I declare that she will not stay hidden under masks or false strength, but rise as the chosen daughter You called her to be.

In Jesus' name, amen.

— Your Sacred Notes —

Diary Encounter: *Sacred Reflection 2*

*(Aligned with Chapter 2 of The Chosen Leah —
The Refining Forerunner, The Almost)*

1. Reflection Hook

Sis, let's keep it real — we've all had an "almost." That job that looked like the breakthrough. That relationship that looked like forever. That opportunity that looked like the door. Almost had you convinced it was the promise… until God showed you it was just preparation. Almost is still not covenant. What in your life once looked like the promise but later proved to be preparation? Write it down — and don't just list it, name the cost of letting it go.

....
....
....
....
....

2. Season Discernment

When you think back to your "almost," what posture best describes where you were in that season?

- **Desperate** — clinging to anything that felt like progress.
- **Distracted** — settling for less because it looked good enough.
- **Hopeful** — believing it might work but unsure.
- **Wounded** — making choices through unhealed pain.

- **Obedient-but-Waiting** — trusting God even as you released it.

Which posture was yours? Why do you think God allowed that almost to happen in your journey?

....
....
....
....
....

3. Deep Dig Prompts

Almosts leave residue — unless you confront them.

- *What drew you to your almost in the first place? Was it security, validation, timing, fear, or desire?*

....
....
....
....
....

- *What red flags or inner checks did you ignore because you wanted it to work?*

....
....
....
....
....

- *What did God refine in you through that almost — and what did you learn about Him in the process?*

....
....
....
....
....

- *What part of you still grieves the almost, and what part of you can finally thank God it didn't work out?*

....
....
....
....
....

4. Prophetic Declaration Space

Now it's time to release the residue of the almost and embrace God's higher plan. Begin here, then add your own:

> *"I will no longer settle for almost when God has promised me more. What looked like loss was actually refining. I release what was never mine, and I embrace the promise that cannot pass me by."*

Now, write your own prophetic declaration. Let it rise from your spirit until you feel peace where there used to be residue.

....
....
....
....
....

5. Scripture Anchors

Proverbs 19:21 — *"Many are the plans in a person's heart, but it is the Lord's purpose that prevails."*

👉 Almosts remind us that no matter how much we plan or push, God's purpose always overrides. What plan, opportunity, or relationship did you try to force that God, in His mercy, didn't allow to stand?

....
....
....
....
....

Isaiah 55:8–9 — *"For my thoughts are not your thoughts, neither are your ways my ways," declares the Lord. "As the heavens are higher than the earth, so are my ways higher than your ways and my thoughts than your thoughts."*

👉 Almosts expose the gap between what we thought we needed and what God knew we needed. Where has hindsight shown you that His higher ways were better than your almost?

....
....
....
....
....

BONUS HEALING EXERCISE

Burying the Almost

Almosts can linger like ghosts if we don't bury them with finality. This exercise gives you a prophetic act of closure.

On the lines below, write a *farewell letter* to your "almost." Name what it was, how it shaped you, what it cost you, and what you learned. Be honest — grieve if you must, but also acknowledge what God refined through it.

Then, at the bottom of your letter, sign your name and date it. This will mark the day you stopped carrying residue.

Afterward, read this aloud:

> *"This almost was never my covenant. I bless it for what it taught me, and I bury it here. I walk forward free, with open hands for God's real promise."*

....
....
....
....
....

Prophetic Prayer for Your Becoming

Father, I thank You for my sister who has faced the sting of almosts. You know every door that closed, every relationship that fell short, every dream that looked right but wasn't Your best. I pray she would no longer carry residue from what was never meant to remain. Release her from the weight of disappointment, and open her eyes to the higher ways You've prepared.

Where she has grieved, give her peace. Where she has questioned, give her clarity. Where she has felt like she missed it, remind her that nothing can cancel what You have ordained. Teach her to see almost not as failure, but as refining. I declare she will not settle for less than covenant, and that her spirit will rise with fresh faith for the promise that cannot pass her by.

In Jesus' name, amen.

— Your Sacred Notes —

Diary Encounter:
Sacred Reflection 3

*(Aligned with Chapter 3 of The Chosen Leah —
The Father Wound, Trading Performance for Promise)*

1. Reflection Hook

Listen, sis — the father wound is sneaky. Sometimes it's straight-up absence. Sometimes it's inconsistency. Sometimes it's presence without nurture. But no matter how it shows up, it whispers the same tired lie: "You have to earn love." Nah. We're not carrying that lie another day. Where did it first take root in your life — and how has it shaped the way you move, strive, or settle? Write it down, and don't hold back.

....
....
....
....
....

2. Season Discernment

When you think about your story through the lens of the father wound, which posture feels most familiar?

- **Striving** — working hard to prove your worth.
- **Pleasing** — bending yourself to keep peace or earn approval.
- **Numbing** — hiding from the ache through distraction or unhealthy coping.

- **Surrendering** — slowly learning to trust the Father who heals.

Which posture describes you, and why?

....
....
....
....
....

3. Deep Dig Prompts

This one may sting — but healing only comes when we face it head on.

- *How did your father's presence or absence shape your view of God as Father?*

....
....
....
....

- *What did you learn to perform for — affection, approval, attention, or survival?*

....
....
....
....

- *Where have you repeated this cycle in relationships, friendships, or even ministry?*

....
....
....
....

- *If God asked you to trade performance for promise, what would you have to lay down today?*

....
....
....
....

4. Prophetic Declaration Space

Performance ends here. Your worth is not earned — it's given. Declare it over yourself. Begin here, then write your own:

> *"I am not what I perform. I am who He calls chosen. The Father's love is not earned; it is received. I release striving and step into promise."*

Now, write your own declaration. Speak it until your spirit believes what your head has doubted.

....
....
....
....

5. Scripture Anchors

Romans 8:15 — *"The Spirit you received does not make you slaves, so that you live in fear again; rather, the Spirit you received brought about your adoption to sonship. And by him we cry, 'Abba, Father.'"*

👉 You are not an orphan — you are adopted. The Father's love cancels fear. Where do you need to stop living like an orphan and start living like a daughter?

....
....
....
....
....

Psalm 68:5–6 — *"A father to the fatherless, a defender of widows, is God in his holy dwelling. God sets the lonely in families…"*

👉 God steps into the gaps left by earthly fathers. Where has He already been fathering you, even when you didn't recognize it?

....
....
....
....
....

BONUS HEALING EXERCISE

Write two letters:

1. **A Letter to Your Younger Self**
   Tell her what she longed to hear but never did. Speak life, protection, and truth to the little girl in you who thought love had to be earned.

....
....

2. **A Letter You Wish You Could Have Received from Your Father**
   Write the words you needed then, even if they never came. Let this be the moment you put language to the absence — and invite God to stand in the gap as the Father who never fails.

Prophetic Prayer for Your Becoming

Father, I lift up my sister who has poured her heart out in these pages. You see every wound she carries, every place she has strived for love, and every silence that has echoed louder than words. I declare that she is no longer bound to performance but anchored in promise. Seal her with the truth that she is Your daughter, fully seen, fully known, fully loved.

Where her earthly father could not, You will. Where she has felt abandoned, You surround her. Where she has felt overlooked, You call her chosen. Heal the little girl inside of her, and strengthen the woman she is becoming. Restore what was broken, redeem what was lost, and rewrite her story with Your love. Let her heart find rest, her identity find security, and her voice rise in confidence as a daughter of the King.

In Jesus' name, amen.

— Your Sacred Notes —

Diary Encounter:
Sacred Reflection 4

*(Aligned with Chapter 4 of The Chosen Leah —
The Mother Wound, Learning to Love a Survivor)*

1. Reflection Hook

Whew, sis — the mother wound is no joke. It's not always about absence; sometimes it's presence mixed with brokenness. Love that felt heavy instead of freeing. Words that cut or silence that made you wonder if you mattered. Let's be real: where has your relationship with your mother taught you to perform, protect, or pretend instead of rest in love? Put it on paper — raw, messy, and honest. God can heal what you're willing to face.

....
....
....
....
....

2. Season Discernment

When you reflect on your mother wound, which posture feels closest to your journey?

- **Caretaker** — you carried her pain as your responsibility.
- **Performer** — you worked to keep her happy or proud.
- **Resentful** — you buried love under anger or distance.
- **Grieving** — you mourned what you never received.

- **Healing** — you are learning to separate her story from yours.

Which posture was yours, and what evidence do you see of it in your life today?

....
....
....
....
....

3. Deep Dig Prompts

This wound requires courage to face. Don't rush it — let the truth rise.

- *What survival patterns did you learn from your mother that you still repeat?*

....
....
....
....
....

- *Where did her story shape you into a caretaker, performer, or protector too early?*

....
....
....
....
....

- *What did you need from her that you never received — and how has that gap shaped your womanhood?*

....
....
....
....

- *If you could separate your worth from her brokenness, what truth about yourself would you embrace?*

....
....
....
....

4. Prophetic Declaration Space

Even survivor-love leaves residue, but you are not bound to repeat the cycle. Begin here, then write your own:

> *"I honor the story my mother carried, but I am not defined by her survival. I release her brokenness and receive God's wholeness. I am free to live as His beloved, not as a survivor of someone else's pain."*

Now, add your own prophetic declaration — one that separates your worth from her wounds and restores your identity in Him.

....
....
....
....

5. Scripture Anchors

Isaiah 49:15–16 — *"Can a mother forget the baby at her breast and have no compassion on the child she has borne? Though she may forget, I will not forget you! See, I have engraved you on the palms of my hands…"*

👉 Even if a mother's love was marked by lack or survival, God promises His compassion never fails. Where have you believed you were forgotten, and how does this verse rewrite that belief?

....
....
....
....
....

Psalm 27:10 — *"Though my father and mother forsake me, the Lord will receive me."*

👉 God is not intimidated by the gaps left by parents. Where has He received you in ways your mother could not?

....
....
....
....
....

BONUS HEALING EXERCISE

Mapping the Legacy

Your mother carried her own story of survival. This exercise helps you honor that reality without carrying it as your own. Take your time here — it may stir deep emotions, but it's also an invitation to release what is not yours and receive what God has placed in your hands.

On the left, list what belonged to *her* — the pain, patterns, or survival habits you've recognized came from her story.

On the right, list what belongs to *you now* — the truths, promises, and new patterns God is writing in your life.

When you've filled both sides, draw a bold line or even write across the middle:

"I release what is hers. I receive what is mine."

Let this act be a prophetic boundary in your spirit: you can honor her journey while still stepping into your own becoming.

What Belonged to Her	**What Belongs to Me Now**
....	....
....	....
....	....
....	....
....	....
....	....
....	....

Prophetic Prayer for Your Becoming

Father, I lift up my sister who has wrestled with the ache of the mother wound. You know the places where love came with conditions, where silence left scars, and where survival became the language of her home. I ask You to separate her identity from her mother's brokenness and remind her that she is fully Yours.

Where she has carried her mother's pain as her own, set her free. Where she has performed for love, let her rest in acceptance. Where she has grieved what was missing, comfort her with Your presence. And where she has honored her mother even through hurt, bless her with double honor in return.

I declare that she is not just surviving — she is becoming. She will carry legacy, not just lineage. Her story will not end in repetition, but in redemption. Seal her heart with Your love, and teach her to walk as a daughter who is deeply known and deeply cherished.

In Jesus' name, amen.

— Your Sacred Notes —

Diary Encounter:
Sacred Reflection 5

*(Aligned with Chapter 5 of The Chosen Leah —
The Covenant Community, My Chosen Family)*

1. Reflection Hook

Sis, let's talk about your circle. Don't roll your eyes — you know the one. The people you text when it's messy, the ones you secretly hope will show up, and the ones you keep around out of habit even though they drain you. God never called you to roll solo, but He also didn't call you to keep counterfeit community. Who's really riding for you — and where have you been tempted to go Lone Ranger because trust feels dangerous? Write it down. Don't sugarcoat it. God can handle the truth.

....
....
....
....
....

2. Season Discernment

When it comes to covenant community, which season best describes you?

- **Isolated** — pulling back because of past hurt.
- **Searching** — longing for belonging but unsure where to plant.
- **Connected** — leaning into the family God has provided.

- **Protective** — guarded in community, never fully open.
- **Rooted** — actively building covenant relationships that sharpen and sustain you.

Which season are you in right now? How can you invite God to grow you into the next one?

3. Deep Dig Prompts

Chosen family doesn't just happen — it's built through trust, vulnerability, and discernment.

- *Who has God sent as "covenant people" in your life — those who truly see you, cover you, and call you higher?*

- *Where have you mistaken convenience for covenant, and what did it cost you?*

- *What fears still make you hesitate to be fully known, even in safe community?*

....
....
....
....
....

- *How has God confirmed that belonging is not optional for you — it's part of your promise?*

....
....
....
....
....

4. Prophetic Declaration Space

You are not alone. Declare it over yourself today:

> *"God has set me in covenant community. I am not forsaken, I am not forgotten, and I do not walk alone. I will embrace my chosen family and honor the ones who sharpen me."*

Now, add your own words of declaration about the people God has called alongside you, and your courage to fully show up in covenant relationships.

....
....
....
....
....

5. Scripture Anchors

Ecclesiastes 4:9–10 — *"Two are better than one, because they have a good return for their labor: If either of them falls down, one can help the other up. But pity anyone who falls and has no one to help them up."*

👉 Where has community lifted you when you couldn't stand alone? Write it here.

....

....

....

....

....

Hebrews 10:24–25 — *"And let us consider how we may spur one another on toward love and good deeds, not giving up meeting together, as some are in the habit of doing, but encouraging one another…"*

👉 Where is God nudging you to step back into community, even if it feels uncomfortable?

....

....

....

....

....

BONUS HEALING EXERCISE

The Circle of Covenant

Draw a circle on the space below. Inside the circle, write the names of the people God has confirmed as covenant for you — the ones who cover, sharpen, and strengthen you. Outside the circle, write the names (or initials) of those who may be close but are not covenant.

Check Your Circle — Mini Prompts

- *Are the people inside your circle sharpening you or draining you?*
- *Have you been afraid to move someone outside the circle because of guilt or fear of loss?*
- *How can you invest more deeply in the covenant ones — and release pressure from those who are not?*

....
....
....
....
....

After you finish, write this beneath your circle:

"Lord, help me honor every relationship rightly — but teach me to invest deeply in covenant."

Prophetic Prayer for Your Becoming

Father, I thank You for the covenant community You are building around my sister. Where she has walked in isolation, surround her with chosen people who will lift her arms when she grows weary. Where she has been wounded by false community, heal her trust and give her discernment to know who is truly covenant.

I declare she will not do life alone. She will walk with people who sharpen her, protect her, and push her toward destiny. Bless the circle You are forming in her life, and let her find the courage to fully show up in it. May her chosen family be a reflection of Your love — and may she never again doubt that she belongs.

In Jesus' name, amen.

— Your Sacred Notes —

Diary Encounter:
Sacred Reflection 6

*(Aligned with Chapter 6 of The Chosen Leah —
Becoming Her Before Him, The Sacred Season of Healing & Becoming)*

1. Reflection Hook

Sis, pause. Before the platform, before the promise, before any him—become her. The healed her. The whole her. The daughter-who-knows-her-Name her. Where have you been tempted to hurry the outcome instead of honoring your becoming? What have you tried to "arrive" at before letting God finish the work in you? Write it down—no filters, no fluff.

....
....
....
....
....

2. Season Discernment

Which posture best describes where you are in this sacred season?

- **Rushing** — trying to skip steps and "arrive."
- **Hiding** — avoiding healing because it feels heavy.
- **Healing** — doing the heart work, one layer at a time.
- **Becoming** — practicing new habits, walking in new identity.
- **Rooted** — secure in God, moving with quiet confidence.

Why did you choose this posture? Where do you see evidence of it in your daily life right now?

....
....
....
....
....

3. Deep Dig Prompts

Becoming is holy work. Let's name what God is forming—and what He's asking you to release.

- *What unhealed habit keeps pulling you back into old versions of you?*

....
....
....
....
....

- *Where have you outsourced identity to outcomes, applause, or attention?*

....
....
....
....
....

- *What boundaries (time, relationships, inputs) will protect your becoming this month?*

....
....

- *Who are you when nobody's watching—and what is God affirming in that secret place?*

4. Prophetic Declaration Space

Start here, then make it your own:

"I choose healing over hurry, formation over performance, and identity over outcome. I will become her before any him, any platform, or any promise. I am the Father's beloved, and He is finishing the good work in me."

Add your declarations below—short, specific, and spoken with authority.

5. Scripture Anchors

Philippians 1:6 — *"He who began a good work in you will carry it on to completion until the day of Christ Jesus."*

👉 Where can you see evidence—however small—that God is actively completing the work in you right now?

....
....
....
....

Ephesians 2:10 — *"For we are God's workmanship, created in Christ Jesus to do good works, which God prepared in advance for us to do."*

👉 What part of your becoming reveals His craftsmanship—and which "good works" is He highlighting for this season?

....
....
....
....
....

BONUS HEALING EXERCISE

The Becoming Blueprint (Lies → Truth → Practice)

Name the lie, replace it with God's truth, and choose one simple practice this week that agrees with the truth.

Lie I Believed	Truth I'm Owning (Scripture/Statement)	One Practice This Week
....	....	....
....	....	....
....	....	....
....	....	....

| Lie I Believed | Truth I'm Owning (Scripture/Statement) | One Practice This Week |

....

....

....

Tip: Keep practices small and doable (e.g., 10 minutes of prayer journaling, no phone after 9pm, schedule therapy, decline one draining invite, speak your declaration aloud daily).

Prophetic Prayer for Your Becoming

Father, I thank You for my sister's sacred season of healing and formation. Teach her to choose becoming over hurry and identity over outcome. Where she has chased arrival, slow her into Your presence. Where she has feared the process, flood her with courage and grace. Remind her that she is Your workmanship—crafted with intention, carried with mercy, and completed by Your faithfulness.

I declare she will not return to lesser versions of herself. She will honor her boundaries, protect her peace, and partner with Your Spirit in the quiet work of transformation. Finish the good work You've begun in her, and let her move forward as the healed, whole daughter You designed—ready for every promise in Your timing.

In Jesus' name, amen.

— Your Sacred Notes —

....

....

....

....

....

....

The New Testament: The Fulfillment

Sacred Reflections 7-12

This is the crossing-over — the season where glimpses of God's "yes" begin to manifest in plain sight. But hear me: fulfillment does not mean arrival, and it does not erase the weight of your becoming. It is not the end of refinement, but the place where refinement and promise walk hand-in-hand.

Fulfillment is covenant realized — not just in what you receive, but in who you've become. It is the joy of answered prayers, but also the humility of carrying them with reverence. It is promise tested, stretched, and lived out in the everyday rhythms of faithfulness.

And remember this: your timing may not look like mine, or anyone else's. Some women step into visible fulfillment quickly, while others walk through years of unseen preparation. Both paths are holy. Comparison will only steal your joy, but trust in God's timing will anchor your soul. The point is not how fast you arrive; the point is staying faithful on the path.

These Sacred Reflections are not about rushing into a fairytale ending; they are about stewarding the promise with wisdom, accountability, and surrender. Whether you're still waiting for fulfillment to appear or already holding it in your hands, this section will remind you: the promise was never the point. His presence is. And when you live from that truth, fulfillment itself becomes a classroom where God continues to teach, refine, and transform you.

— Prophetic Declaration —

"This is my season of fulfillment. I will not idolize the promise, nor compare my journey to another's. I declare that my fulfillment is not my arrival — it is covenant with God made visible. I will carry what He gives me with reverence, steward it with wisdom, and remain surrendered to His presence above all else. My yes is in Him, not in the outcome."

Diary Encounter:
Sacred Reflection 7

*(Aligned with Chapter 7 of The Chosen Leah —
The Promise in Plain Sight, Enter Will)*

1. Reflection Hook

Sis, let's talk. Sometimes the promise can be standing right in front of you and you won't even recognize it—not because you're blind, but because God is still preparing your eyes to see. Hidden doesn't mean absent. Delayed doesn't mean denied. Write honestly: where in your life might God already be moving, but your heart hasn't caught up yet?

....
....
....
....
....

2. Season Discernment

Which posture sounds most like your heart right now? Circle one, then tell why.

- **Guarded** — protecting yourself from disappointment
- **Distracted** — busy enough to miss what's already near
- **Healing** — learning to trust again, vision still tender
- **Unaware** — sensing God is near, not sure how

- **Trusting** — leaving unveiling to God's timing

Why that posture—and what do you think God is protecting or preparing in you?

....
....
....
....
....

3. Deep Dig Prompts

Sometimes God hides the promise to protect it—and to grow you.

- *Where might God be moving in your life right now, even if you can't fully see it yet?*

....
....
....
....
....

- *If you do have hindsight, where do you now recognize His mercy in the waiting?*

....
....
....
....
....

- *What expectations (how it "should" look) could be blinding you to how He actually works?*

....
....
....
....
....

- *What might God be protecting you from by keeping certain things veiled for a while?*

....
....
....
....
....

4. Prophetic Declaration Space

Speak this aloud, then add your own:

> *"God is faithful even in what I cannot yet see. Hidden is not forgotten. Veiled is not void. What You've promised will be unveiled in Your perfect time—and I will recognize it."*

Now write your declaration of trust and alignment.

....
....
....
....
....

5. Scripture Anchors

Habakkuk 2:3 — *"For the revelation awaits an appointed time; it speaks of the end and will not prove false. Though it linger, wait for it; it will certainly come and will not delay."*

☞ Delay isn't denial; it's appointment. Where are you being invited to wait with faith?

....
....
....
....
....

Isaiah 40:31 — *"But those who hope in the Lord will renew their strength. They will soar on wings like eagles; they will run and not grow weary, they will walk and not be faint."*

☞ Strength is formed in the waiting. How is God strengthening you while things are still veiled?

....
....
....
....
....

FULFILLMENT PRACTICE

Tuning Your Receiver (3-Day Micro-Practice)
God doesn't always speak the same way twice. This practice trains your discernment *now*—no hindsight required.

Day One — Word
Ask God for a scripture to sit with today. Write the phrase that arrests you and why.

....
....
....
....

Day Two — Whisper
Sit in silence for 10 minutes. Pay attention to peace, a nudge, or a gentle correction. Note what you sense.

....
....
....
....

Day Three — Witness
Invite one trusted, godly voice to pray and share what they perceive. Record confirmations or redirects.

....
....
....
....

Seal It — One-Sentence Alignment
Today I choose to tune my hearing to how You're speaking now:

....
....
....
....

Prophetic Prayer for Your Fulfillment

Father, I thank You for the way You prepare Your daughters to step into promises at the right time. For my sister, I pray she would not be anxious about what she doesn't yet see, but confident in Your timing. Give her discernment to recognize when You're unveiling what has been hidden. Teach her how to carry fulfillment with wisdom, not fear; with gratitude, not entitlement. May she rest in the truth that when the promise is revealed, she will be ready—whole, rooted, and anchored in You.

In Jesus' name, amen.

— Your Sacred Notes —

Diary Encounter:
Sacred Reflection 8

*(Aligned with Chapter 8 of The Chosen Leah —
Look at God, A Test of Faith)*

1. Reflection Hook

Sis, let's be real — God will wrestle you when you'd rather wiggle out. You've tried to keep control, set limits, or bargain with Him… but He doesn't let you slide. He presses you past comfort because He knows your calling requires more. Think about it: where has God been stretching you, refusing to accept your shortcuts, and holding you accountable to the "yes" you gave Him? Write it down.

....
....
....
....
....

2. Season Discernment

When you think about your current walk with God, which word best describes the posture of your season?

- **Wrestling** — arguing, resisting, struggling to release control.
- **Surrendering** — shaky but choosing obedience one step at a time.
- **Obedient** — walking it out even when you don't fully understand.

- **Refined** — learning from what He shut down.
- **Expectant** — beginning to sense the promise flagging you down.

Which posture was yours? Why do you think God has you in this place?

....
....
....
....
....

3. Deep Dig Prompts

These aren't surface-level questions. Let God press on the real places.

- *Where have you tried to set limits on God — telling Him what He can or cannot ask of you?*

....
....
....
....
....

- *What "almost" were you tempted to cling to, even though God already said no?*

....
....
....
....
....

- *What did obedience cost you in that season — and what did it unlock in your spirit?*

....
....
....
....
....

- *Where might God already be flagging your promise, even if your eyes aren't fully open yet?*

....
....
....
....
....

4. Prophetic Declaration Space

Now it's time to declare the blessing that follows obedience. Speak this aloud, then expand it in your own words:

"I will not fight God's hand — I will yield to His refining. What looks like wrestling is actually His love. I release what He has closed, and I trust that my true promise cannot pass me by. When the timing is right, I will see it clearly."

Now add your own declaration. Prophesy over your season until peace rises above the wrestle.

....
....
....

5. Scripture Anchors

Genesis 32:26–28 — *"Then the man said, 'Let me go, for it is daybreak.' But Jacob replied, 'I will not let you go unless you bless me.' … Then the man said, 'Your name will no longer be Jacob, but Israel, because you have struggled with God and with humans and have overcome.'"*

👉 Wrestling with God doesn't disqualify you; it transforms you. Where is He changing your name, your identity, or your outlook through the struggle?

....
....
....
....
....

Hebrews 12:11 — *"No discipline seems pleasant at the time, but painful. Later on, however, it produces a harvest of righteousness and peace for those who have been trained by it."*

👉 God's discipline is proof of His fathering love. What "painful no" or "hard push" have you faced that is producing peace and righteousness in you now?

....
....
....
....
....

FULFILLMENT PRACTICE

Wrestle, Release, Recognize (3-Day Micro-Practice)

This practice slows you down so you can see God's mercy in the process. Take it step by step over three days:

Day One — Wrestle

Write down one area where you're still wrestling with God. Be raw about the resistance. What don't you want to give up? What feels unfair?

....
....
....

Day Two — Release

Come back and name what "almost" or false option you need to let go of. Write a farewell to it — even if it's just one sentence.

....
....
....

Day Three — Recognize

Finally, ask God to show you where He's already flagging your promise. Write down any whispers, nudges, or quiet confirmations you sense — no matter how small.

....
....
....

Prophetic Prayer for Your Fulfillment

Father, I thank You for my sister who has wrestled with You and chosen obedience over comfort. You see every place she resisted, every "almost" she was tempted to cling to, and every step where she finally surrendered. Cover her in grace for the stretch, and remind her that the wrestle is proof of Your love, not punishment.

Where her eyes still feel veiled, unveil them in Your timing. Where she fears missing the promise, assure her that what You've ordained will not pass her by. Let her know that blessings wait patiently, flagging her down, until she's ready to recognize them. I declare that she will not confuse almost for covenant, distraction for destiny, or comfort for calling. Her obedience will open doors no man can shut, and her fulfillment will arrive right on time.

In Jesus' name, amen.

— **Your Sacred Notes** —

Diary Encounter:
Sacred Reflection 9

*(Aligned with Chapter 9 of The Chosen Leah —
Love is in the Air, Acceleration Begins)*

1. Reflection Hook

Sis, let's keep it a buck—how many times does God have to highlight the same thing before you stop calling it coincidence? The scripture that echoed your prayer. The "random" conversation that landed too perfect. The sign that showed up right when you needed it. Sometimes God isn't whispering; He's shouting. Where has He been dropping breadcrumbs you brushed off? Write it down—confirmation isn't random, it's covenant in disguise.

....
....
....
....

2. Season Discernment

When confirmations show up, they meet us in different postures. Which one feels most like you right now?

- **Skeptical** — brushing off signs as "just life."
- **Hopeful** — you want to believe, but you're cautious.
- **Nervous** — afraid to misread God's voice again.
- **Expectant** — ready to receive, even if you don't fully see how.

- **Grateful** — recognizing His mercy in even the smallest reminders.

Why that posture? What might God be protecting or preparing in you through it?

....
....
....
....
....

3. Deep Dig Prompts

Slow down. Notice how He confirms—and how you tend to respond.

- *What is one recent "too specific to be random" moment you're tempted to call coincidence?*

....
....
....
....
....

- *Where might fear of past mistakes make you cautious about current confirmations?*

....
....
....
....
....

- *What assumptions about timing or method could be blinding you to how God is actually moving?*

....
....
....
....
....

- *If you treated these signs as mercy instead of mystery, how would your response change this week?*

....
....
....
....
....

4. Prophetic Declaration Space

Now it's time to align your mouth with what God keeps showing you. Begin with this declaration, then expand it in your own words:

"God, I will not dismiss Your confirmations as random. I will slow down, pay attention, and honor the ways You speak to me. Every sign You send is laced with love; every nudge is rooted in mercy. I choose to align with Your timing."

Add your own declaration. Let your faith catch up with your sight.

....
....
....
....
....

5. Scripture Anchors

Isaiah 30:21 — *"Whether you turn to the right or to the left, your ears will hear a voice behind you, saying, 'This is the way; walk in it.'"*

👉 God doesn't just call from a distance; He directs in the moment. What is He whispering that confirms the way forward?

....

....

....

....

....

Ecclesiastes 3:11 — *"He has made everything beautiful in its time. He has also set eternity in the human heart; yet no one can fathom what God has done from beginning to end."*

👉 Confirmation without timing can confuse. Where is He asking you to trust His timing even as signs increase?

....

....

....

....

....

FULFILLMENT PRACTICE

Confirmation Compass — Reflection Guide

This Reflection Guide is designed to help you slow down and gather what God is highlighting in this season. Use it as a way to name the confirmations you've noticed and align them with His Word and your next step of obedience.

A. Signals (What showed up?)
List 3–6 recent "breadcrumbs" (signs, phrases, scriptures, conversations).

....
....
....
....

B. Scripture (What agrees with the Word?)
Write 1–2 verses that resonate with those signals (include a phrase that hits your spirit).

....
....
....
....

C. Witness (Who confirms?)
Note any godly counsel or inner peace that aligns (or cautions).

....
....
....
....

D. Step (What obedience looks like this week)
Name one clear, small act of obedience that honors these confirmations.

....
....
....
....

E. One-Sentence Alignment
Today I choose to respond like this:

....
....
....
....

Prophetic Prayer for Your Fulfillment

Father, thank You for confirming Your heart until our doubts run out of excuses. For my sister, sharpen her discernment and steady her courage. Let her recognize Your voice in the loud signs and the quiet nudges. Teach her to honor confirmation as covenant, not coincidence, and to move at the speed of Your timing without fear. May every breadcrumb guide her steps, and may her obedience open into the beauty You've appointed.

In Jesus' name, amen.

— Your Sacred Notes —

....
....
....
....
....
....
....
....
....
....

Diary Encounter:
Sacred Reflection 10

*(Aligned with Chapter 10 of The Chosen Leah —
God's Plan, From Courtship to Covenant)*

1. Reflection Hook

Sis, let's not get it twisted — acceleration isn't a fairytale montage with a soft filter. It's messy, stretching, and sometimes terrifying. When you're finally in season, God can move so fast your head spins. But speed doesn't mean skipping process. Acceleration still demands surrender, faith, and wisdom. Don't romanticize the suddenly. Receive it, steward it, and let it sanctify you instead of scare you.

2. Season Discernment

When you think about your current walk, which season sounds most like where you are? Circle one:

- **Waiting** — still lingering in promises you've yet to see.
- **Accelerating** — things are happening fast, almost too fast.
- **Harvesting** — you're holding fruit you once prayed for.
- **Grieving-after-Acceleration** — what came quickly also brought unexpected loss or stretching.

Now, write why you chose this season. How is God showing you His pace in this part of your story?

....

....

3. Deep Dig Prompts

Acceleration presses the yes out of you. Let's dig deeper.

- *Where have you felt God's invitation to move quickly, even when fear wanted you to hesitate?*

- *What lost years or seasons do you sense He's beginning to redeem?*

- *How do you tend to romanticize acceleration — imagining ease without weight? What truth is God teaching you instead?*

- *If acceleration also meant stepping into both promise and pressure at once, what would trust look like for you?*

....

....

....

....

....

4. Prophetic Declaration Space

Read this aloud first, then add your own words:

> *"This is my season to trust God's pace. I will not romanticize acceleration, nor fear it. What looks sudden is His redemption at work. I receive His timing, His order, and His glory — even when promise and pressure arrive hand in hand."*

Now, write your own prophetic declaration about acceleration in your life.

....

....

....

....

....

5. Scripture Anchors

Amos 9:13–15 — *"Yes indeed, it won't be long now. God's Decree. Things are going to happen so fast your head will swim—one thing fast on the heels of the other. You won't be able to keep up! Everything will be happening at once—and everywhere you look, blessings!"*

👉 This is God's signature suddenly: when sowing and reaping collide. Where have you seen Him shorten the distance between planting and harvest?

....
....
....
....
....

Joel 2:25 — *"I will repay you for the years the locusts have eaten…"*

👉 Acceleration isn't random. It's God paying back what felt wasted. Which "lost years" do you believe He's redeeming in your story?

....
....
....
....
....

Isaiah 61:3 — *"…to bestow on them a crown of beauty instead of ashes, the oil of joy instead of mourning, and a garment of praise instead of a spirit of despair."*

👉 Sometimes acceleration and ashes arrive together. Where is God asking you to hold both — the beauty and the burden — as part of His redemption?

....
....
....
....
....

FULFILLMENT PRACTICE

Open Hands, Open Heart

Acceleration is about stewardship. What you grip too tightly can break. What you release to God, He multiplies.

On this page, use the open-hands graphic as your guide. In the open space between the hands, write the blessings, opportunities, or breakthroughs God has placed in your reach. Let it symbolize what you're entrusting back to Him.

Beneath the hands, write a short prayer of stewardship — releasing control and asking God to teach you how to carry acceleration without losing intimacy with Him.

Sample Prayer of Stewardship

"Lord, I release these blessings back into Your hands. Teach me not to cling in fear or pride, but to carry with wisdom, humility, and grace. Multiply what I place before You, and let my acceleration bring glory to Your name."

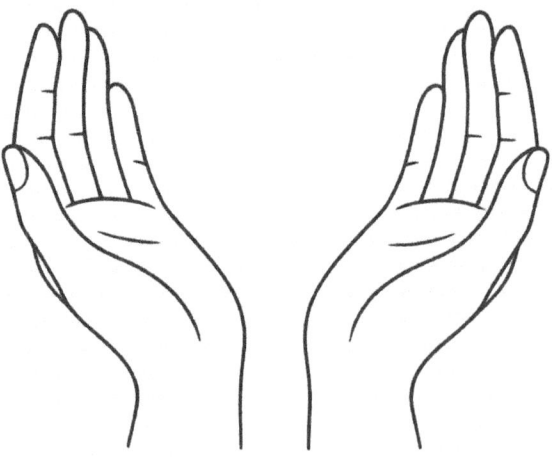

....

....

Prophetic Prayer for Your Fulfillment

Father, I thank You for my sister who longs to see Your hand move in her life. Remind her that Your timing is never late, and when You accelerate her path, it is not to overwhelm her, but to redeem what was lost. Teach her to trust both the beauty and the burden of the suddenly season. Strengthen her to run at Your pace, not her own. Guard her heart from fear, comparison, or romanticizing the process, and give her courage to embrace the weight of glory that comes with acceleration.

I declare she will see the Amos 9 harvest, taste the Joel 2 redemption, and wear the Isaiah 61 beauty-for-ashes mantle with strength. Let her story become living proof that Your timing is perfect and Your redemption complete.

In Jesus' name, amen.

— Your Sacred Notes —

Diary Encounter:
Sacred Reflection 11

*(Aligned with Chapter 11 of The Chosen Leah —
The Space Between: Bleeding Promises & Bruised Expectations)*

1. Reflection Hook

Let's be real — giants don't vanish just because you've crossed into the Promised Land. Sometimes they get louder. Sometimes they bleed into your joy, bruise your expectations, and leave you wondering if this was really the promise after all. But sis, hear me: even here, God is not testing your worth — He's testing your willingness. The altar is where He cuts the temptation to idolize the promise and calls you back into deeper obedience. Are you willing to surrender even what He gave you, trusting that He knows how to resurrect it? Write about the giants you're facing in your "fulfilled" place — the grief, the warfare, or the disappointments that make you question what God already confirmed.

....
....
....
....
....

2. Season Discernment

Even in fulfillment, you may feel pulled back into refining. Circle what best describes your "space between" right now:

- **Wrestling** — fighting giants that feel bigger than your strength.

- **Weary** — holding grief or disappointment while trying to stand in faith.
- **Surrendering** — bringing your promise back to the altar, even when it hurts.
- **Obedient** — leaning into God's instruction, even when it cuts against your comfort.

Why did you choose this word? What evidence do you see in your season that confirms it?

....
....
....
....
....

3. Deep Dig Prompts

Sis, this is the trench work — the questions that strip away pretense and push you toward obedience.

- *Where have you been tempted to romanticize acceleration, assuming it would mean ease instead of testing?*

....
....
....
....

- *What "giants" are showing up in your promise, and how have they bruised your expectations?*

....
....

- *What part of you wants to cling to control — and what would it cost to place that on the altar?*

- *How is God asking you to obey Him in a deeper way through this season of wrestling?*

4. Prophetic Declaration Space

Speak this aloud until your heart begins to believe it:

> *"My promise is not my idol. I lay it back on the altar, trusting God to sustain what He started. The giants in my land will not define me, the bruises will not break me, and my obedience will unlock the blessing. I am not forgotten, I am fortified."*

Now extend this in your own words — what do you need to declare about obedience, surrender, or faith in the "space between"?

5. Scripture Anchors

Hebrews 11:17–19 — *"By faith Abraham, when God tested him, offered Isaac as a sacrifice. He who had embraced the promises was about to sacrifice his one and only son… Abraham reasoned that God could even raise the dead, and so in a manner of speaking he did receive Isaac back from death."*

👉 Sometimes the truest faith is not in receiving the promise but in laying it back down. Where is God calling you to trust Him with your Isaac?

2 Corinthians 10:4 — *"The weapons we fight with are not the weapons of the world. On the contrary, they have divine power to demolish strongholds."*

👉 When the warfare feels personal, remember it is spiritual. Where have you been tempted to fight in the flesh, and how can you instead hand the battle to God?

FULFILLMENT PRACTICE

The Altar Exchange

In this exercise, you'll place your "promise" back on the altar. Not to lose it, but to remind your heart that God is the Giver and Sustainer.

- **Above the word ALTAR:** Write what you're laying down — your bruised expectations, your disappointments, or even the fear of losing what God gave you.
- **Below the word ALTAR:** Write what you are trusting God to resurrect — joy, peace, faith, intimacy, restoration.

Prophetic Prayer for Your Fulfillment

Father, I lift up my sister who stands in the space between bruised expectations and bleeding promises. You see her weariness. You know the giants she faces in her fulfilled place. Remind her that obedience is not loss — it is life. That surrender is not weakness — it is worship.

Teach her to place every bruise, every burden, every battle on the altar, knowing You are faithful to sustain what You began. Where she feels unseen, be her Witness. Where she feels depleted, be her Strength. Where she fears letting go, remind her that resurrection is Your specialty.

I declare that she will not idolize the promise, nor crumble under the weight of it, but rise in deeper obedience, stronger faith, and greater intimacy with You.

In Jesus' name, amen.

The Pause Before the Crown

Sis, breathe. We've walked a long road together. You've traced your sacred mess. You've faced the almosts, wrestled the wounds, and laid masks at the feet of God. You've carried the weight of survival, sifted through legacy, and chosen honesty over hiding. That was the Becoming.

Then came the Fulfillment — acceleration that left you dizzy, confirmations that whispered and shouted, blessings you almost didn't recognize because your eyes were still adjusting to promise. You've said yes when fear tried to choke you, released what you wanted to grip too tight, and even carried your promise to the altar when God asked for it back. That's not weakness. That's obedience. That's faith forged in fire.

And now… here you are. The hallway before the stage. The pause before the crown. You've been stretched, bruised, refined — but you're still standing. Still saying yes. And that yes has brought you here.

Picture it: the doors haven't opened yet, but you can hear the murmur on the other side. The stage is lit. Heaven's applause swells like a sound you can't quite describe. Your name is about to be called. Not because you were perfect, but because you were willing. Because you stayed. Because you let God write through your life what you never could have scripted on your own.

This is the moment when surrender shifts into commissioning, when faithfulness is crowned, when obedience becomes legacy. The crown waiting for you isn't ornamental — it's authority. It's responsibility. It's the weight of being trusted to carry impact beyond yourself.

So pause. Let this holy hallway remind you: every tear, every stumble, every whispered prayer — none of it was wasted. God has been shaping you for such a time as this. And sis, don't you dare freeze now. You didn't come this far just to stop in the hallway. Don't trip — the crown's waiting.

Before You Step Out...

What fear, doubt, or lie do I need to leave here in the hallway so it doesn't walk onto the stage with me?

....
....
....
....
....

What truth from God do I want to carry in my spirit as I step into legacy?

....
....
....
....
....

If heaven gave me one sentence to declare before the crown rests on my head, what would I say?

....
....
....
....
....

Ready, Queen? It's time. I'm right here with you — let's step out together.

Diary Encounter:
Sacred Reflection 12

*(Aligned with Chapter 12 of The Chosen Leah —
A Chosen Leah, Marked by Obedience, Mantled for Legacy)*

1. Reflection Hook

Sis, coronation looks good on you. You've walked the hallway, laid it all on the altar, and now you stand on the edge of legacy. Let's make this plain: a mantle isn't just a "churchy word." It's a covering of authority, a God-given assignment, the weight of a calling wrapped around your life. A mantle says, **"You carry this now — not for your glory, but for God's kingdom."**

Today, you are stepping onto the stage of obedience. Not because you were flawless, but because you were faithful. You didn't earn this mantle by perfection; you received it because you said yes. And now, your yes becomes seed — carrying weight far beyond you, stretching into generations you may never meet.

2. Legacy Activation

This isn't about looking back — it's about looking forward. Take time to write into the future:

- *What mantle do you sense God has placed on your life?*

....
....
....

- *What legacy do you long to leave through your obedience?*

....
....
....
....
....

- *Who will be impacted because you said yes?*

....
....
....
....
....

3. Prophetic Declaration of Coronation

Speak this aloud over yourself, then extend it in your own words:

"I am a chosen daughter, marked by obedience and mantled for legacy. I will not shrink back. I will not compare my journey. I embrace the mantle on my life and walk boldly in my assignment for such a time as this."

Now, add your own coronation words below. Write the decree that heaven and earth will recognize as your mantle statement.

....
....
....
....

4. Scripture Anchors

Esther 4:14 — *"And who knows but that you have come to your royal position for such a time as this?"*

☞ Esther didn't feel ready or qualified, but her obedience shifted nations. Your mantle carries weight for more than just you.

Revelation 12:11 — *"They triumphed over him by the blood of the Lamb and by the word of their testimony…"*

☞ Your testimony is not just survival; it's a weapon. What you've walked through becomes a victory cry for others.

Ecclesiastes 12:13 — *"Fear God and keep his commandments, for this is the duty of all mankind."*

☞ Legacy isn't built on gifts alone, but on consistent obedience. What you practice in private will echo in public.

FULFILLMENT PRACTICE

Crown & Commission

This is your coronation moment. You'll see an image of a crown being lifted in ready hands. In the open space beneath the crown and between the hands, write the legacy you choose to carry forward. Let it be specific: words God has spoken, names you are called to cover, assignments He has entrusted to you, or promises you are commissioned to steward with faithfulness. Fill that space as a declaration of what your "yes" will release for generations to come.

Then, beneath the crown, finish this sentence:

"Because I said yes, my legacy will be…"

....
....
....
....
....

Prophetic Prayer for Your Legacy

Father, I thank You for my sister standing at the threshold of legacy. She has wrestled, surrendered, and said yes. Now, mantle her with boldness. Let her obedience mark her, let her testimony commission her, and let her legacy multiply through generations she may never see.

I pray she would carry this mantle not as a burden, but as an honor — a sign that heaven trusts her voice, her story, and her obedience. Where fear once silenced her, let faith amplify her. Where shame once bound her, let legacy break forth.

I declare she is mantled for legacy, chosen for such a time as this, and commissioned to walk in her divine assignment with courage and joy.

In Jesus' name, amen.

— Your Sacred Notes —

✦ Closing Declaration ✦

*I have walked through wilderness and promise, through
breaking and becoming.
Every tear has been counted,
every yes has been seen.
I rise — marked, mantled, and made for legacy.
I am Chosen.*

Daughter of Promise,
let this page be the seal of your journey.
The promise is alive within you.

LeahVaDol
KIRK

Website: www.leahvadolkirk.com
Instagram: @the.chosen.leah
Facebook: LeahVaDol

www.ingramcontent.com/pod-product-compliance
Lightning Source LLC
Chambersburg PA
CBHW040231110526
44582CB00001B/10